AUREUS SOL

Sad People Love Sad Music

First published by Sol House Productions 2022

Copyright © 2022 by Aureus Sol

All rights reserved. No part of this publication may be reproduced, stored or transmitted in any form or by any means, electronic, mechanical, photocopying, recording, scanning, or otherwise without written permission from the publisher. It is illegal to copy this book, post it to a website, or distribute it by any other means without permission.

Aureus Sol asserts the moral right to be identified as the author of this work.

First edition

This book was professionally typeset on Reedsy.
Find out more at reedsy.com

Contents

Bob the Builder prequel

I still smell you in my hair
  I still picture your face there
  Holding up my hair
  Picking me up from the chair I've adhered to
  Dusting me off

I know you like to pull my bones apart just to put me back together
  Bob the builder prequel, master of destruction

Now you're picking out what I'll wear
  Dress me up, I'm your baby doll
  Looking through your eyes like you know me
  I still feel your hands imprinted on me
  My skin is a ghost town
  Covered in tombs and gravestones

You, with your empty set of eyes and needy hands
  Even at the end we cannot rest in peace
  Blood on my white sheet
  Tonight we'll go out scaring kids
  Trick 'r treat from the grownups

Trick 'r treat in reverse
Halloween came early
Honey go and get your money from your mom's purse

Another fucking lifetime, can you find what's missing?
You never even stop to say hello anymore
This is old news
Very, very old news

not even a friend

If I died today
Could you honestly say that you tried
You weren't even like a friend to me
You cut ties like I just weighed too heavy

I don't know how many times you think you need to tell me you don't want me
Are you really trying to convince me or yourself

Lately I feel like I don't really need anyone anymore
Lately I tell everyone I don't think I need anyone anymore

You say that I'm a liar
I keep my secrets to myself
In the darkest of the night I pray I won't die by myself

I answer the phone too many times in the middle of the night
I am only a corner for you to toss at all the shit you don't really need

Is it really dark out or is it only your eyes
You tear apart a rosy start to end it with a blank slate

Flip back the pages until I know you less
Rip out the words until there's nothing left

In my heart
Shit's still a mess
I fight to be alone but I know you best

Putting myself to the test
Poured it all in
There was nothing left

I'm not what you think of me
I am not bad news
I am not a bad guy

You can't tell that I'm fine
But they say I'm alright
I feel like I'm dying every fucking night

Shots fired
I could blow my brains
You wouldn't stop me
I am only there for you
How fucking exhausting

endless nights

At night I became terrified
   Like the sun would never come to rise

a shell

I still have dreams of cutting myself up in my room
  Take another pill
  I pray that I will die soon

The drugs die off
  I wish I did too
  I still have dreams of cutting myself up in my room

A clean state I can paint red
  Nobody understands the shit that's in my head

Darkness climbs in like a fucking bandit
  Steal the sun with a gloved hand

And I pray to god
  I pray there is a god

I'm sinking beneath something I can't even see
  And I hide from everyone who says they love me

Drink every last drop of blood
  Call it love

A SHELL

I hand you every piece of me and it's not enough
When I have nothing left to give
You turn your back on me
Leave me breathless
Leave me without a will to live

Well take any bit of me
I am just a shell of all I said I was going to be

Take any piece left of me
I am just a shell of everything I said I was going to be
I am only remains of dreams
I am only dust

at night

Think about it at night
  Think of how I want to die
  Think about it at night
  Wishing I could end my life
  Think about it at night
  Feelings I can't keep inside

leech

It's about how I can't feel it even the sun
It's about how when I wake I wish the day was done

Drink every last drop of blood in me
You won't rest until you have what's left of me
I see you now
You're like a leech
You're a parasite
Why should I even try
Or even fight
You'll never stop
You'll never have enough
You need me empty
You need my life to suck

I can't take away this pain in me
I think the doctor should put another brain in me

I know you see the monster inside
Why try to run
Why try to hide
I give every inch of me

holding on for hope

Each day I feel less
  Each day you're more like a stranger

Holding on just for hope
  What a danger

breathing underwater

DROWNING

No one knows what it's like to try to breathe underwater
I'm so far under
I swim towards the light
I'm only sinking farther

sleeping for a thousand years

I'm dreaming of sleeping like a thousand years
The hardest thing I've ever done is live a life when you weren't here
What's a life worth living when you've lost your own damn mind
Leaving you behind
I left part of who I was
I left my own soul behind
Maybe it was the bravest thing
Maybe I'm the weakest link

old habits

I'm in the depths of depression now and I don't really want to come out
It's familiar
Like an old habit you can't seem to break
I think I'll stay

puzzle piecer

We trade eyes but no words
On earth I'm falling off the ground
I was desperate to need somebody who could stick around
If it's only in my head I tell myself you're someone I can cling to
Hanging onto something beautiful like the thought of you
Holding onto the edge of what I thought was the whole world
I've been blind but see
If there was a chance I could repay you
I'd give you my last breath
If I sound desperate well I once was
From a distance you spotted my missing pieces
Collecting them like wild fruits you bring me myself
Gently
Gently
Piece by piece
I am pieced back together by your soft hands
A puzzle piecer
You look me in the eyes
And everything falls into place around me
And I'm falling for you undoubtedly
We speak in silence

Glances and gazes is all we've needed
Everything's falling into perfect alignment
I'm too familiar with the waves of your skin to really turn me back now
If I lean into you could you really have my back now

If I needed something to cling to
Could it be you
There's a lot that we could say
Talking
Nothing's filled with words
Something's always in the way

comfort isn't safety

Wrapping up in the blackness of it all
There's comfort here
My eyes adjusting quicker with the lights off
There's comfort here
Like sleeping in the room you used to cut your skin in
There's comfort here
Like how the blade finds that old mark
A familiar groove
And you press down without thought
A familiar move

paranoia

I feel paranoia from everyone
Even my momma
Laughter fills the room when I walk out of it
I am just a show to put on for you
I am nothing but a joke
You know as well as I do

comfortability

There is comfortability in the silence
In my head it's never quiet

a place to call home

Desperate for feeling
Wrote like a sad song I need you near to me
When we touch
Breathe life into me
If I ask you
Would you play along
I had to believe you had all the answers
Tearing at your skin
Rip at the seams
Searching for something I've felt my whole life missing
I need something I can rely on
Like a place where I can hang my hat up and lay my head down
Like a place where I can breathe and feel like a peace around me
You carve me a key to your heart so I have a place to call home

first sight

I just met you so I pretend I'm not in love

parade of horrors

Can I rest now and say I tried
I tried my best
I can't continue to bleed out
I only try to bandage you
You need every bit of my light
I'm turning to dark
You cut out my heart
Serve it to yourself on a platter
What will it take to get out of here alive
Bullet wounds stain my skin
I've been away at war for a lifetime
I give you everything I am and there's no part of me left to hang on to
I don't even see me anymore
I'm dying for you to be okay
You lead me in chains down into my grave
Everyone's cheering
We're leading the front of the parade

up for weeks

If you'd just go with your instinct
It doesn't think
So why do you so much
Can I reset my mind
Go back in time

At night
Need to get my hands on some pills
So I can get some sleep
Voices in my head keep me up for weeks

pain to ease the pain

Wondering how something so sharp can dull the pain

light sucker

Life sucker
  Light sucker
  You need me to light you up
  When you leave I turn to dust

retired soldier

I need things to be easy now
I need to rest my head when I walk around
I've been at war for a lifetime now

line dry

Hang me up on a line to dry
  I've had enough endings for a thousand lifetimes

skin and bones

Skin and bones
  I hold your skin and bones close so I feel close

even when I'm fine

I miss you all the time
Even when I'm fine

I know you won't be fine without me

I don't try to forget you
Brown eyes lighting up under street lights
And I know you saw me
When you didn't want me
You broke my heart in two
I needed you like a reason
Keep my head up and keep breathing

Now I just try to sleep at night
Now I just have to try to sleep at night

Voices in my head
I'm doing just fine

I try to trust you're safe
I know you're not fine
Please be alright
Please be alright

I had to keep going
You needed me but no longer could you hold me

comfort in change

Thinking about days ahead and I am not afraid
I used to find comfort in the pain now it's in change
I didn't want to outgrow you but you needed me to
Meet you where you are
I had to leave you where you are
Well I pleaded
I did my best for you
I had it all on the line
I gave my life to you
You pushed me all alone like what was I to do
I tried to stay and wait
You drank for weeks we couldn't sleep here

visitors in my head

The voices in my head aren't even mine
They devour me with clawed hands

a caring stranger

I am someone who cares
Like I check your table when you walk away
Make sure you didn't leave anything behind

weathered and numb

You lead me on
I blindly follow
I lay myself out there
Naked
Completely exposed
You take pieces of me as they fit you and I hand them to you softly
The more you light up the more gray I become
Weathered and numb
I hate who I become
Weathered and numb
I hate who I become
Weathered and numb
I hate who I become

and I will love you then, and then

I am someone who will understand exactly what you have to say
without you speaking a word
I am someone who will know exactly where to lay my hand
upon your face
so that you feel like you can breathe again
I am someone who will love you
even when you're screaming at 4 A.M. for me not to

hopeless as the rest of them

I hope
What a joke

the absence of me

How was I so easy to not miss
How was my absence something so easily covered
You move around it like you don't even notice

How could you have been so in love and now you're out of it
I keep falling deeper and it's been so long since I've even seen you

the only thing easy for you was leaving

Do you feel the pain the same
Is it only in my brain
I thought I left a mark on you only you're still pale and it's me who's bruised
I thought I'd make a difference
You didn't even notice when I was there
I thought you needed me around
When I packed my bags you didn't make a fucking sound
You said loving me was easy
The only thing easy for you was leaving
I beg you to change your mind
You just turned your back
I thought you'd miss me
You haven't even noticed that I'm gone
Was it really that easy to just play along

a hundred times

A hundred times an hour
  I'm climbing over your shoulder
  You called me over and then you're turning your back

Crying about it
  Crying about it

Said that I was fine without you
  Say it a hundred times just so you can't tell I'm lying to you

seeker not see-er

Yes
I
Try
To find the light
But it doesn't mean I see the day

golden girl

You made me feel golden
  Like the sun was shining on me even in the nighttime

meant for this

He says he loves the way I fit
Like maybe our bones were meant for this
Maybe our lips were meant to kiss

my name

Damn
I miss
How you
Would say
My name
Just to hear
Me
Say yours

retired dreamer

I used to dream
  I used to have dreams
  Now they're just nightmares
  I wake up from night terrors

too small to last

It wasn't enough to last
Maybe I had lacked in strength or size
I laid down everything
After a year, a series of months, or so
You'll forget me
Have you already started

fooled by lines

You told me I was keeping you alive
  What a lie
  What a line
  Fool me
  Every time

in the sun

I missed you even when the sun was shining- especially when the sun was shining

feral

They think I'm not meant to be wild because I don't have fur or sharp teeth

No one really took the time to try and know me
I was sitting there itching in your sweater
Feeling more constricted than in a straight jacket

I need more alone time than you think

I need some time to breathe
I had to hold mine through the crowd
I'm sorry it's been taking so long

I know we only have so long

You told me to hang on
Just be strong, just be strong
I know we only have so long

Nowadays that makes me sad when it used to make me glad
I want to live forever now
I guess that's a good sign

waking up without you

I haven't slept through the night in weeks
My throat feels raw when I wake up from screaming
I've been seeing you in my dreams and when I wake up
I am reaching for your ghost
I watch you fade before me as the sleep leaves my eyes
This is terrifying, terrifying
You used to tell me that you loved me more than life
How was I to know you were just lying

life sucker

You suck the life from me like you need it more than I

enjoy it while you can

Thankful for the good times even though they never last

stranger in my bed

I CAN'T EVEN LOOK YOU IN THE EYES ANYMORE

worth the pain

I lied
  I don’t regret anything

I'll live in memories now

If I'm sleeping, I'm dreaming, don't wake me
I could live inside my head forever, with you, I'd be fine with it
If we could re-live the whole time or just rewind a bit

my head is my enemy

I'm only important if they need me
  It's only meaningful if they notice me

If I don't earn it I don't deserve it

I'm not allowed to take up space unless they ask me

notice me

Lately I'm just trying to impress you
  It's all for you
  And if you don't notice anything then it's all for nothing

I want you fucking inside of me
  You can't even touch me

kill me for attention

You cut me with your knife and I'm bandaging you
 Light me on fire and I'm putting you out

I must go, I must go

Please
  Try to understand my desperation
  I must go
  I must go now
  In this kind of world I feel no peace
  I've found no home

who are you

Sometimes I wake up and you don't look like even a friend to me

just to prove I’m right

I am afraid I will do anything to prove that you will leave me eventually
   Cause everyone leaves
   Eventually

fly on

We fly on
Please fly on

What are we searching for
What are we fighting for
Is it really out there
Somewhere
If I search high and low if I search around the globe will I ever find what I'm looking for

There once lived a child in me
She hoped hopes, dreamed bigger dreams
Stronger though, more like a fighter than me

Mom always told me I could be everything
Mom can I still be anything I want to be

Can I pass the stars and make the moon
If I keep them to myself will my wishes come true

more than

I love you more than everything I love added up together

being in love makes me dreams of trees

I love each part of life
As long as I'm awake I can find something to love
I crave sunrise to sunset lying tangled in you in our bed
Lips pressed longingly down your skin
You need me to let you in
I'm dying to
I dream up of days lost among trees
Bare earth beneath my feet
I'd move along like the wind stirring leaves
Climbing to the tops and swinging branch to branch
I want to feel the breeze guide my body
I want to belong to the air
Floating, maybe flying
Speed picks up and I am higher
I am one with the sky
Somewhere else a clear sky, a dark night
Too many stars I lose count
And when I tip my head back I feel like they could swallow me whole

feeling is my compass

I just want you to be serious
I lack in comedy
I move with my feelings like a needle in a compass
I'm drowning in them or starving from the lack of them I feel from you
You can't care
I'm crying
Mostly crying
But it feels a whole hell of a lot like dying

heavy

My muscles can no longer bear the weight of my bones

fooled them all

Out on my own
No one really hears from me
And that makes them think I'm doing well
I guess they really fell for it this time

nocturnal

I know you like me to see you with the lights turned out
Keep me in the dark
Hide your scars from me
I asked for your heart like you could take it all apart for me
Unbreakable walls don't cave, they leave fingers bruised

anchors don't save drowning people

I still feel your light dear
  While the earth swallows me whole
  I'm captivated but blind, near
  I hear you calling for me
  I said I'd never leave here
  I'm hanging on just for hope
  I cling to your lines but they're tightropes for me
  I've lost sight and I fall
  Throw your love like an anchor to me
  Around my neck I just choke

So long
  I wanted to tell you everything
  Now my secrets have a key

beautiful

Every morning
I'm so in love
It drives me mad
The entirety of my being is consumed in the feeling of it
You are so beautiful
I can't stop staring

There is a parade of wild animals dancing in my body
You are breathtaking
Painstakingly beautiful

magnets

Pull me in
Attract me like a magnet
Add up every thought I've had
Nothing compares
I'd release myself of everything
You mean more than anything

This is like an addiction

I can't break my body away from yours if I wanted to
I'm glued
Stuck to you
I can't get enough
We're never close enough

worshiper of darkness

Darkness creeps in again
Takes over my head
Claims territory
Takes control
And I am like a worshiper
A loyal follower

all-consuming

No one really knows love like I love
  All-consuming

sad sounds

I am shaking in my bones
Through the streets I walk you home
You close the door
The saddest sound
Goodbye never said aloud

everything

You are everything
  Everything
  With you I can't long for anything
  Anything
  I feel complete
  I am not only where I want to be
  I am where I need

purple skies

Purple skies
Wanted to die
If the moon could change your mind we picked a perfect night to go outside

Dark eyes
Tell me lies

Like I love you more
Or there's a green floor
Below a purple ceiling

And I'm planting seeds
So trees will grow beneath me

There's comfort for a shadow in the shade
Say my name I feel okay

I love you more
I know I know
It feels terrifying
Terrifying

Lose myself in you and it feels like I’m dying

rainbow mind

They said it wouldn't take so long
  So long
  I get tired of people always telling me to be strong
  I've been strong
  They tell me just to think of rainbows in my mind I'll be fine

stop sign

Does it all come to an end when I'm dead?
Will there be a stop sign in my head?
The pain gets to me again
I can't continue
To care
When I don't have the means to
I used to dream of dreams
Now I just dream of peace

I once was blind

Nothing feels as dark anymore
  Even through the clouds I see the sun
  Less than sinking, more like floating
  At last, relief, a sense of peace
  Glowing, flames, inside of me
  My spark re-lit and now I see
  Shining, brighter, endlessly

I once was blind, now light I see

nothing to do but cry

Sometimes I feel like nothing
And if I don't ever do anything extraordinary no one will ever notice me
And I just feel meaningless
Life is pointless
No one would notice if I would just leave this

Who knew nothing would feel so much like something
A darkness encompassing the entirety of my being
My existence
It's dark and I feel nothing
I feel nothing and it's dark

So I just cry
I just cry
Tears falling from my dead eyes

I'm on my way

I was lost among the chaos, you were my guide along the way
Floating, flowing, through endless commotion
Like gravity, you grounded me
It isn't enough to say you gave me an escape or a home base
You brought me back to myself
I was lost
But now I'm on my way

All around me it is madness but within you I find stillness
All inside me there is darkness but in your light I feel just fine

lean on

I feel it all
Like shards of glass piercing through my skin
I feel your pain, it's what I'm in
Tugging on my heart, until it's unraveling like string
You can close your eyes, pretend it's fine
I feel it just the same

I didn't want to see it
But I had to look that way
I didn't want to see it
But there was no other way

There's darkness at the bottom
And the weight will keep you sinking

Take a load off, baby
Tell me your secrets, give me your mind

If it wasn't me, who would it be?
You're strong, I know
You don't have to show me
Nothing to prove, lay down your defense

I'll carry you on
Lean on, lean on
I'll carry you on
You don't have to be strong

how can life be over when I'm not dead too

Maybe we should pay more attention
Soon I'll be gone and you won't mention me again
To you
Or any of your friends
We share a life together
But I guess that ends too
But how can life be over when I'm not dead too?

Hang me up
On the line
I've told you this
A thousand times
Waiting for a life that is never mine

There are some things that we'll forget to mention
You wanted heart and my affection
I needed time and your attention

are you whole now

If you're done let me know

You wanted me when you were alone
  Do you feel whole now

my own worst enemy

I am growing tired
I write apologies
Say I'm sorry
Fuck it up and do it all again
My worst enemy is me

just think of me

I don’t want to take up your time
  Just your mind

life that was never mine

Everything good
  I don't deserve it
  I should leave it all behind
  You call it life but it was never mine

Let's just get away
  Nothing's permanent anyways

fill me with your touch

Fill me up
  I’m empty inside
  Touch me
  I can almost feel you

where will I go when you don't need me anymore

And when you don't need me anymore then where will I go?
Did you plan for that?
When you feel whole on your own?
When you don't need me to complete you
any longer
I'll go back to where I came from
Like I'm untouched
And you're not bothered
Am I really making a change?
Am I making you stay?
Or just keeping your days until you can see again?
And when you don't need me anymore then where will I go?
Did you plan for that?
When you feel whole on your own?
When you don't need me to complete you
any longer
I'll go back to where I came from
Like I'm untouched
And you're not bothered
Am I really making a change
Am I making you stay?

Or just keeping your days until you can see again?

where’s your head

Do you feel the distance

When you’re near
   Where’s your head
   Are you even here?

time moves quick when you're not looking

Life moves quick
Time it slips
Not everyone places the same value on a minute or a day
Sometimes it takes more to appreciate the same
Here is what I know: when you're counting the numbers, the change is so slow
Lose yourself in the moment and it's over before you know

a life in my mind

How I feel is my reality
  I don't need your validity
  You can keep your truth away from me

When the morning comes
  If I'm still sleeping
  Then I'm dreaming
  Don't wake me
  I've been thinking about just staying here
  A life in my mind could fit me just fine

A blissful ignorance

nothing to see

I'll be here but another minute
  I wish you could've seen just how much my heart was in it
  If it makes no difference I'll take my things and leave
  It wasn't really something to see, you have to believe

no words

Beyond knowing
  Beyond thinking
  All that is is feelings and within them I'm consumed
  We don't really have the words but they're all we have to say
  I needed an escape and you swept me away

my heartbeat drives me insane

Scratch the thoughts out of my brain
You will never understand how I forget the pain
It takes more than we will ever admit to ourselves
If I give you a piece of mine will you keep me alive
Cause I don't really need you more than you need me
My family wants my heartbeat but all it does is drive me insane

phantom limbs

You can't cage a thing when nothing is for free

Your touch so cold
All I want is to go
All I want is not to know
How it feels
All I think, is how it feels
Haunted, I feel your imprint ingrained
Fingers burned into my skin
Let go, I plead, for release
At night your face won't let me sleep
I live inside of nightmares
I've never had a dream
Have you heard of phantom limbs?
Like when your leg's cut off but you still feel it's presence?
Like a ghost that won't let go
In the dark a shadow will always follow
Take your fucking hands off of me
I'm not yours, you can't own me
Like a tattoo or a scar
I try my hardest to forget your marks on my skin
A broken tape stuck on repeat

Voices echo inside my mind, nowhere to turn, nowhere to hide
Get me high, keep me numb, the only way to stay alive
These thoughts they run loops in my head
I need an escape, they never end
Leave me on my own it's all I know

need to forget

Sometimes I just want to die
Nothing matters at all
Happy or sad
Good or bad
I can't escape what's in my head
Will I ever fucking forget
Can't get through a day if I'm not high
I just want some peace and quiet in my mind
Being numb is the only way
Wake me from this nightmare
Release me from this hell

insecurities eat me

How do I explain weird thoughts in my brain
If I told you everything then you'd label me insane
I've been paranoid, I'm sorry
There's voices in my head
I've been feeling like they haunt me
Sometimes it's like I can't separate fantasy from reality
My insecurities eat at me and I can't even breathe around you
I'm always watching my moves
Every step I make I do a double take
I've lost some parts of me I'll have to recreate
I need some reassurance, some confidence
Lately I've been worried that all I do is wrong
I'm self-conscious every time the lights turn on
Forget about me all I want to do is please you
All along, I'll go along
I need you just to need me

praying for rain

Nothing is coming in clear in my head
  Everything looks blurry
  Everything feels fake

What are we even here to do if not just ache and wait?

Maybe I should have played it safe
  I was in a rush
  I tried to hurry up not wait
  Love, it comes and goes
  In waves
  Sometimes you're sinking deeper in it
  Then you're praying for the rain
  Tonight I want to drown in you
  But you're running out out of sea
  Love, I guess, doesn't flow in abundance, at least not for me

not my world

If you tell me to leave, then I'm leaving
This world's really not for me
No matter who's around me, I'm still feeling lonely
No matter where I go, I never feel at home

I needed you
I don't need anyone

nothing ever stays the same

I know you thought I didn't mean it
But every night I'm fighting demons
I know you need a reason not to leave
We never sleep
Sinking deeper into you, and you in me
I know you didn't believe me
Now I need you more than you need me
You tell me you won't leave but I know how things change
Nothing lasts forever, nothing ever stays the same

fights lost to yourself

In the middle of the night we lose the fight

If my arms are bleeding
  I'm my own worst enemy

living to die

I didn't want to stay but I had to
Everyday I say I'm not going to make it through but what's new?
They told me to hang on so I held you
When things get bad in my head again I wish I was dead again
I wrote them all a line, said I'm sorry, you'll be fine
Hang me up to wait
All I want is to escape
There's a pain deep in my soul, they might have to operate
Some of us put up a fight, some of us just live to die
We can't find a reason why so we just kill time
Until the end, waiting for the end
The only thing that we can count on
The sun rises each day, as I lie here awake
The sun rises to wake, I'm still lying awake

rewind everyday

Slow down, don't blink
If I could I'd stop time or
Live every moment with you on repeat
If I'm sleeping I'm dreaming
Don't wake me
With you, I find my meaning
Any minute could last forever
I don't mind it
If I could rewind, relive everyday
I'd be fine with it

I love you more

Love is flowing through my veins
 In my dreams I see your face
 In the morning I love you more than me
 In the morning I love you more

addicted

He is light
He is love
He is everything
I touch
I cannot get enough
I crave his skin just like a drug

www.ingramcontent.com/pod-product-compliance
Lightning Source LLC
La Vergne TN
LVHW050317160826
845677LV00014B/3441